audience of one

audience of ONE

BEHOLD THE LAMB

CALEB WAMPLER

CONTENTS

1

THE CROWD

Today's society is all about building who you are, building your brand, expanding your following, becoming bigger and better, more recognized, and more known. Everyone is looking to increase their influence in their communities. Because of this pursuit, and the endless platforms of social media, it would seem that the culture is all about bigger and better. Everyone is trying to increase their social following because they are trying to expand their reach. The further your reach, the bigger the influence you have, and with a big influence comes a bigger *audience*. Your *audience* is who is paying attention to what you have to say and do. The more people that are listening to you, the more influential you have the potential to be.

The Bible is chock-full of examples of the Lord raising up people unexpectedly, take Queen Esther for example. It's full of stories of the overlooked becoming people of prominence. I love the example of King David. He was a young shepherd boy, yet God elevated him to lead a nation. It's full of spectacular displays of heavenly power like was often seen in the life of Moses. We read all of these stories, yet there's something so overlooked by people today. It's the simple message that our loving Savior Jesus is wooing the hearts of people. What if our need for speed, our drive for popularity, our symbols of status, our pursuits of power, and our ideological quests were all laid down upon an altar? What if instead of filling the stadiums of our lives with people we are trying to speak to, and favor we are trying to gain from a crowd, was boiled down to the AUDIENCE OF ONE that we had the opportunity to minister to.

PICTURE THIS...I can almost see it now...

You plan for weeks for the presentation of your lifetime. You get all of your best thoughts on to paper. You prepare the most epic presentation of all-time. You invite every major player who has ever played any role in your life. You make reservations at the best venue, and invite anyone you had ever wanted to meet to advance your goals, and to make your dreams come true. You go through weeks and months of preparation, and the day finally comes for your big moment.

As you enter through the back door of the venue, your palms begin to sweat, and butterflies fill your stomach. Everything you have ever wanted to see happen could all be fulfilled in this moment. The passions you've carried, the dreams that have filled your heart, and the hopes you longed for have all come down to this moment. As you move from the back hallways and enter onto the stage behind the curtain, your heart is racing and you start to have second thoughts. You check to make sure you've got your notes and presentation ready. Then you realize the time has come. As you walk from behind the curtain, everything is suddenly revealed, and you're absolutely stunned at what you see!

In the giant room, there is only one person sitting there. All of your hard work, all of your invested time and energy, all of your blood, sweat, and tears have come to this turning point in your life. Your fears, hopes, anger, excitement, and ego all come down to this defining moment of your life. As your emotions boil in the gut, they rise into your chest, and the deepest cry comes bellowing out. What comes out stuns you, stops you in your tracks, and even surprises you.

"It's you! You came! Behold the lamb! Lord Jesus, you're here!" As you run off the platform, you nearly trip and fall. He chuckles, and you run into His arms for the sweetest embrace. He holds you tightly and says, "I've been waiting for this moment all your life. I'm so glad you came. I was waiting for you."

If that was a little bit of a plot twist for you, then perhaps this book has been written from the heart of heaven just for you. I want our focus to go back to an *audience of one.*

With all that could be said and done in your life, there is really only one thing that matters. As King David himself wrote in Psalm 27:4, "The one thing I ask of the Lord – the thing I seek most – is to live in the house of the Lord all the days of my life, delighting in the Lord's perfections and meditating in His temple." The beauty of Jesus, and the simplicity of His beckoning of our hearts is the thing that matters. Our knowledge of Him, and His knowledge of us...the relationship building...the history we build with God...little by little...day by day...moment by moment...is what levels you up in this life. You won't even realize it's happening as you become something the world is not worthy of, like we read in Hebrews 11:38. "They were too good for this world, hiding in caves and holes in the ground."

In Acts 2, the very first Christian gathering that ever took place came out of the Upper Room. We know that Jesus died on the cross, was raised from the dead, and before He went into the heavens, He told the disciples, "Do not leave Jerusalem, but wait for the gift my Father promised, which you have heard me speak about." (Acts 1:4) The disciples waited in anticipation for the coming of the Holy Spirit. Eventually, the Holy Spirit came out of Heaven and baptized them in fire and gave them new tongues. They had fire over their heads, similar to the burning bush with Moses. This was a beautiful and amazing moment where they experienced the power of God. Following this infilling of the Holy Spirit, Peter stepped up and gave the very first Christian message in the history of Christianity. Jesus told Peter before that he would be the rock that the church was built on.

"And I tell you that you are Peter, and on this rock I will build my church, and the gates of Hades will not overcome it. I will give you the keys of the kingdom of heaven; whatever you bind on earth will be bound in heaven, and whatever you loose on earth will be loosed in heaven." (Matthew 16:18-19)

Peter stood up and gave his first message that drew crowd participation. If you have an *audience of one,* then you only care about what *He* thinks, says and does. John 5:19 says, "Jesus gave them this answer: "Very truly I tell you, the Son can do only what he sees his Father doing, because whatever the Father does the Son also does."" If Jesus only did what He saw the Father doing, or only spoke of what He heard the Father saying, then shouldn't we be doing the same thing? So often, we gather a crowd around us, and we get them to say what our ears want to hear. We build up a following to tickle our ears because it sounds and feels good. But as Peter began to minister, he began to hear a variety of different responses from the crowd.

The first reaction found in Acts 2:12 was that some were *perplexed.* Why were they perplexed? I am not positive, but I do know that some people are confused about everything in life. Some people are perplexed by the way you should drink coffee. Some are perplexed at how to style their hair or decorate their house. Some are perplexed by what movie or show they plan to watch. No matter what you say or do, there will be people that are perplexed by what you say and believe. They will be puzzled about everything and everyone, and you can guarantee things will be that way until the day we breathe our last breath.

The second reaction from the crowd, coming from a different group of people, was mocking Peter. Acts 2:13 says, "Some, however, made fun of them and said, "They have had too much wine." No matter what, people are going to mock you, what you believe, what you say, or what you do. And even more so with the things of God. People will mock *everything* you do. If you don't believe me, just take a look at your social media accounts for the night. Turn on the news for a few minutes, and you'll quickly find one person mocking another. Go to a family reunion and the chatter will turn to the word-of-mouth commentary about something pretty quickly. In our faith, people will quickly mock everything from our belief systems, to the way we raise our children in the Lord, and even to the things we feel the Lord leading us to do. Why? Because it is what people do.

There is a third set of people in this passage that had a different reaction entirely. There were those that *believed*. In Acts 2:41 we read, "Those who accepted his message were baptized, and about three thousand were added to their number that day." Three-thousand that were saved that day! That is a pretty good first day in the office, isn't it? Not many people have seen that many people come to the Lord in one day. The crowd of thousands and thousands was trimmed down to three-thousand, because people were perplexed and could not understand what Peter was saying. It was foolishness to them. They could not understand that unschooled and ordinary men had been with Jesus. Acts 4:13 says it this way, "When they saw the courage of Peter and John and realized that they were unschooled, ordinary men, they were astonished and they took note that these men had been with Jesus." The disciples were a little bit different, but God used them to change the world. We are able to preach the Gospel today because God used these men so long ago. As an Evangelist who travels the world preaching the Gospel in mass-crusades, I'm happy to designate this as the first recorded crusade in church history!

In Judges chapters six and seven, Gideon, the youngest of his tribe and least of all of the clan, was selected by God to lead a revolution. He rose up in chapter seven of Judges, and he and the army stood up against the Midianites. He had thirty-two thousand troops, and the Bible says that they were outnumbered four to one. I do not think anyone would want Gideon's job that day. He was the weakest and the least, but Gideon was chosen by God for another purpose that he couldn't see yet. Gideon's response was telling God, "We need more troops, please send more." And God's response was, "No, you need to get rid of some of them." Gideon must have responded with, "Are you kidding me God? This is the worst plan ever. Our men barely know who I am, and I have no experience in battle. I'm the least, worst, and weakest, but you want me to get rid of men, even when we are outnumbered?" Ultimately Gideon decided to follow the plan of the Lord. He said "Anyone who is afraid right now, go home." The Bible says that twenty-two thousand people left that day, so ten-thousand troops were remaining. Before the men left, they were outnumbered four to one. Now they were outnumbered twelve to one!

If there are people in your life who are constantly speaking fear into you and surrounding you with negativity, it's time to mute these voices from your life. What I care about is hearing the *audience of one* and what He has to say. The thousands and thousands that Peter preached to were cut down to the three-thousand that believed. Similarly with Gideon, he was cut down to ten-thousand men but God again tells him, "You have too many people." He then sends them to the river for a test. Some men go down to the river and throw their shields and swords down and scoop water from the brook to drink. These men were careless of their surroundings, so this is how God trimmed the army again. He separated the ones who scooped the water with both hands, possibly exposing themselves to the enemy, from the others who drank from the brook another way. He sent everyone but three hundred men home. He cut the army down to those who believed they could actually do something, and he put everything on the line to follow what God wanted through the least likely source.

2

JESUS IS YOUR
AUDIENCE OF ONE

God is reducing things down to an audience of one. He is asking, "Are you willing to trust me in spite of life not being like it used to be? Some are wondering if things will ever get back to normal after the covid pandemic took the world by storm. As churches, restaurants, and sports arenas across the world emptied out, we are only now beginning to see some things resemble the way they used to be. And I emphasize, *only some things*. Where many received their validation from the masses in the past, those masses, in many cases, are no longer around. The measure of success and fulfillment can no longer be attained through the crowds. In this process, I feel the Lord has given us the most perfect of opportunities to search our hearts to see if He is really the prize of our lives.

A very unlikely victory came through Gideon, and he was appointed to become the commander of the area he was in. Gideon's family was restored, and everything ended up being great for him and his nation of Israel. What is it that God has asked you to do, and what are you doing to steward His voice in your life that others do not believe that you are called to do?

In John six, we find the historic story of the feeding of the five-thousand. Most scholars would quickly point out that there were probably fifteen to twenty-thousand people, including the women and children. In the story, Jesus takes the fish and loaves of bread from a little boy, breaks them, and feeds the multitude. I can only imagine what the Pharisees were saying.

In this passage, Jesus quickly realizes all these people are starting to follow Him for the good natural things that come with Him. Maybe you'd find yourself in the same situation seeking God to gain His blessings, looking for Him to prosper your life. I mean after all, why wouldn't you go to the countryside and follow a man who is going to pour His life into you, provide amazing teaching, and cover your appetite with some free food? Within days, there was a following around Jesus, consisting of people who were wanting to coast by and hear the most popular word of the day. His new trendy followers saw this powerful minister taking care of their needs, and it moved them to shout forth in John 6:14, "Surely, he is the

Prophet we have been expecting!" As we keep reading, verse fifteen says, "When Jesus saw that they were ready to force him to be their king, he slipped away into the hills by himself."

In those days, Jews were oppressed by the Romans and were in bondage as slaves. There was political tension and stress that all the people tangibly felt. There was immense pressure on Jesus to speak a message that they wanted to hear and tickle their ears. They wanted Jesus to tell them He was the Messiah they'd been praying for, and that He would free them from the Romans. Jesus sensed that these people were in it for their own personal and political gains. Sure, who wouldn't want to be free from their oppressors? However, it was *all* they wanted.

They just wanted a handout. They weren't in it for the Kingdom of God that Jesus was there to establish in them and through them. Maybe if you searched your heart for a moment, you'd find yourself in the same place as these people from so long ago, searching for a God of politics, a God of blessing, a God of prosperity, a God of healing, and a God of free handouts. It would be good for us to do a spiritual assessment and see where we fall present day in our here and now. This is how Jesus handled the situation. "Then Jesus declared, "I am the bread of life. Whoever comes to me will never go hungry, and whoever believes in me will never be thirsty. All those the Father gives me will come to me, and whoever comes to me I will never drive away. For my Father's will is that everyone who looks to the Son and believes in him shall have eternal life, and I will raise them up at the last day. Very truly I tell you, the one who believes has eternal life. I am the bread of life. Jesus said to them, "Very truly I tell you, unless you eat the flesh of the Son of Man and drink his blood, you have no life in you. Whoever eats my flesh and drinks my blood has eternal life, and I will raise them up at the last day. For my flesh is real food and my blood is real drink. Whoever eats my flesh and drinks my blood remains in me, and I in them. Just as the living Father sent me and I live because of the Father, so the one who feeds on me will live because of me. This is the bread that came down from heaven. Your ancestors ate manna and died, but whoever feeds on this bread will live forever." (John 6:35, 37, 40, 47-48, 53-58)

Remember, at this time, when He spoke these words, He had not died on the cross yet, so people were confused by what He was saying. On hearing this speech from Jesus, the disciples responded with "This is a hard teaching. Who can accept it?" (John 6:60). Now we have commentaries and teaching on what these verses mean. People can openly debate and come to a conclusion on Jesus' words. But back then, He was regarded as a man who seemed to be the new local prophet in town who told them to eat His flesh and drink His blood. They did not understand Him and told Him that it was a hard teaching that no one would accept. Even though He was supplying their needs, they were perplexed by what Jesus was saying. But Jesus snapped back when He became aware of their grumblings by asking, "Does this offend you? Then what if you see the Son of Man ascend to where he was before! From this time many of his disciples turned back and no longer followed him." (John 6:61-62, 66)

They were following Him because they wanted to be free from the Romans, but He started to fine tune what His mission was, and proposed to them that they follow Him for the sake of the Kingdom. This drove them away, so Jesus looked at the twelve disciples and asked them, "You do not want to leave too, do you?" (John 6:67). Peter's famous response was this, ""Lord, to whom shall we go? You have the words of eternal life. We have come to believe and to know that you are the Holy One of God." Then Jesus replied, "Have I not chosen you, the Twelve? Yet one of you is a devil!"" (John 6:68-70).

Jesus was not just trying to build a big following in these verses. He was trying to establish the truth of the Kingdom of Heaven, that you have to go to Him to receive life. You do not get life from anywhere else. Jesus says in John 14:6, "I am the way and the truth and the life. No one comes to the Father except through me." You cannot receive life from social media inspirational quotes, from how big your following is, how big your platform is, how many awards you've received, how big your salary is, how powerful your position is, from your degrees, from your family, from your friends, from your boss, from your spouse, or from a host of other seemingly good things. None of these other things are Him!

He may lead you to things in your journey, but they are not a replacement of Him. He is the prize all along. We never graduate from Him!

You must crucify yourself on your cross daily, pick it up and follow Him wherever He goes. These are the people God is looking for in this season. He is pruning the crowd so that He may prepare His bride. He is pruning the crowds, and testing the motives of individuals so that He may see who his true disciples are. He is going to find His core and then going to offend them a little bit. Does Jesus offend you? He is trying to find the offense in your heart and in this generation. God is doing a work in those who will stay with Him no matter what.

Doing things to please other people will lead to nothing and be unfulfilled. Doing what pleases God will lead you to life. Your life is about an *audience of one*. There will always be hecklers, naysayers, critics, mockers, those who are careless, those who are in fear, those who are perplexed, or following you for a handout. There will always be people who attach themselves to you because they are afraid and want to coast off of someone who is not as afraid as they are. The Lord is pruning and shaking all these people because He does not want our value to be found in humanity, material possessions, status, or symbols, but only in Him. If you find value in everything else, then you will be valueless. The value of your life comes not from humanity and what others say, but from your secret place and what God says. If you care about everyone's opinions all of the time, and that is what motivates you in this life, then you will never be fulfilled.

Obedience is a byproduct of somebody who has counted the costs, above all else, to follow Jesus. What is God asking you to do? I have a feeling that, today in this world we are living in, everyone is trying to find the latest celebrity ministry, the most famous quotes, and the best way to grow in numbers, stature, or prestige. But instead, let's bury our knees in our carpets, and pray to the One who gives us our fresh assignments for the Kingdom of Heaven. Let's raise up and release the angel armies of Heaven against the powers of Hell from our bedrooms. We need a people in this day and age, that when God looks at them asks, "do I offend you?" we respond with "please Lord, see if there is any wicked way within us. We repent of our sins and only desire Your voice. You matter above all else." When He tries to prune everyone and everything out of our lives, can He look at you and prune you? Will we answer saying, "We embrace it Lord, do whatever you want, even if it hurts or is uncomfortable?"

"Then they came to Jericho. As Jesus and his disciples, together with a large crowd, were leaving the city, a blind man, Bartimaeus (which means "son of Timaeus"), was sitting by the roadside begging. When he heard that it was Jesus of Nazareth, he began to shout, "Jesus, Son of David, have mercy on me!" Many rebuked him and told him to be quiet, but he shouted all the more, "Son of David, have mercy on me!" Jesus stopped and said, "Call him." So they called to the blind man, "Cheer up! On your feet! He's calling you." Throwing his cloak aside, he jumped to his feet and came to Jesus. "What do you want me to do for you?" Jesus asked him. The blind man said, "Rabbi, I want to see. Go, said Jesus, "your faith has healed you." Immediately he received his sight and followed Jesus along the road." (Mark 10:46-52)

Jesus walked into town and blind Bartimaeus was there and started saying, "Jesus, Son of David, have mercy on me!"

Bartimaeus realized that this was where he could get his healing. No doctor could heal him, no government could assist him, there was no one that could help him but Jesus. While he was calling out to Jesus, many rebuked him and told him to be quiet, but he shouted out to Jesus all the more. As the crowd rebuked and ridiculed him, he kept up and tried harder to get Jesus' attention. Jesus stopped and said, "call to him." How did the crowd respond? They told Bartimaeus to cheer up and get up because Jesus was calling for him. If you just go by the opinion of those around you, and only care about their opinions, you will become unbearably empty, sick, and broken. God is doing a great work inside of each of us, but we must embrace the suffering and pain. We have to be willing to stand in the gap for an entire generation, you have to be willing to go where no one has gone before, you have to do what no one else has done. We must press into His presence and the person of Jesus. As Luke 6:45 says, "For the mouth speaks what the heart is full of."

You may ask, am I doing this? Am I following what everyone else is shouting at me? Or am I following Christ? There is a saying, show me where your bank account is, show me what your schedule is, and I will be able to tell you what is important to you. You could do the same with your internet interactions and posts. What are the last twenty posts you have made? What are the last twenty texts you sent? What are the last twenty emails you sent? Who were the last twenty people you called, and what were you talking about with them? If you assess your life and conversations, then you will know what your heart is full of. I encourage you to do this right now as we conclude this chapter. Don't go to chapter three until you've done this.

You may be surprised at what you find. Maybe you already have a feeling what you're going to find out when you do this. Either way, my question for you is simple. *Is Jesus and His plans, purposes, words, and promises flowing from your mouth?* Or is it something completely different? Is it people's opinions, the latest news story, or the latest trending topic on social media? Perhaps it's what someone recently said to you about you? Perhaps it's a passion that has consumed you, or a topic that you've devoted your time to.

No matter what it is, is it saturated and inundated with the presence and purposes of God? If not, it's time to get back in your secret place, and pour out your life at the feet of Jesus. If life is the sum of the decisions we make daily, is there any fruit pointing to the fact that you've been with Jesus? If not, may this be a wakeup call to return and present yourself before the only One found worthy! The abundance of your heart will begin to overflow with worship and adoration to your **AUDI-ENCE OF ONE!**

3

THE ONE THING

We are entering into a moment of inspection from the Lord. Man looks at the outward, but the Lord looks at the heart. 1 Samuel 16:7 says this, "...The LORD doesn't see things the way you see them. People judge by outward appearance, but the LORD looks at the heart." Man looks at the outward display of the leaves, but we are now entering an inspection time of the root.

While many will cast their attention upon numbers, popularity, promotional materials, videos, photos, one-liners, and a plethora of other prestigious recognitions, the Lord is focused on the oil of the secret place. *I heard the Lord clearly speak that the time for gathering oil before His return is coming to its close.*

In Matthew 25, it says this:

"Then the Kingdom of Heaven will be like ten brides-maids who took their lamps and went to meet the

bridegroom. Five of them were foolish, and five were wise. The five who were foolish didn't take enough olive oil for their lamps, but the other five were wise enough to take along extra oil. When the bridegroom was delayed, they all became drowsy and fell asleep. "At midnight they were roused by the shout, 'Look, the bridegroom is coming! Come out and meet him!' "All the bridesmaids got up and prepared their lamps Then the five foolish ones asked the others, 'Please give us some of your oil because our lamps are going out. "But the others replied, 'We don't have enough for all of us. Go to a shop and buy some for yourselves.' "But while they were gone to buy oil, the bridegroom came. Then those who were ready went in with him to the marriage feast, and the door was locked. Later, when the other five bridesmaids returned, they stood outside, calling, 'Lord! Lord! Open the door for us!' "But he called back, 'Believe me, I don't know you!' "So you, too, must keep watch! For you do not know the day or hour of my return." (Matthew 25:1-13)

Friend, we are in the final hour before the great and glorious return of our Lord and Savior Jesus Christ! It is the most crucial hour of preparation that the world has ever known. You see, right now, the Lord is watching and inspecting the roots of His beloved bride. He's preparing her for His return for her beautiful wedding day.

As He implements His end-time harvest plan, He is calling to and awakening a generation of mighty champions who have been found ready and waiting. He is revealing Himself in the secret place to those who have taken the time to gather oil in their lamps. He is filling their lamps to the brim. He is taking those who have chosen with their own free will to INVEST it into Him and His presence. It's costly. It's time-consuming. It's sacrificial. It's expensive. It can even be humiliating, and it is oh so precious and holy.

AW Tozer is known to have said this, "To desire revival and at the same time to neglect personal prayer and devotion is to wish one way and walk another."

As the Lord inspects our roots, He is pruning us. Oh, the pain and joy of this excruciating process of becoming more like Jesus. It's this very process that allows the full expansion of the root system for the full weight of what He is about to display in the earth upon it.

The prophets have spoken for decades of a coming billion soul harvest of an end-time revival of an outpouring of the Spirit prophesied in the Bible in Joel 2:28 and Acts 2:17. The days of the outpouring of God's Spirit are upon us and are knocking at the door. He will fall with fire upon those who have oil in their lamps, ready to be a lamp that is kept burning, and whose fire will not go out.

In a recent time of prayer, I heard the Lord say that He was about to reposition and remove some who have masqueraded as anointed. It isn't even that they weren't anointed or haven't walked in the gifts they were given, but that in the spotlight of pressure that has been upon them, that some have coasted off of a previous season of oil. For these, they are dangerously close to empty. The repositioning or removing will depend upon their heart posture to return to the secret place and love Him as their first love again. The choice is theirs.

I also heard the Lord say that He will advance His secret place champions into places of prominence and prestige. Watch for these warriors to rise from obscurity into political offices, leading roles in Hollywood, to places of financial influence, and to become kings and prophets in their spheres of society. Wickedness will rise during the same timeframe, but those found ready in waiting, will be promoted by the living God as Esthers in our generation. Their fame will come as a voice of opposition to all that the enemy plans to do. Perhaps, it will be YOU.

What is the oil? Friend, it is the oil of intimacy with Jesus. It's Jesus. John 1:29 ESV says, "Behold, the Lamb of God, who takes away the sin of the world!" He's the only one found worthy to open the scroll in the book of Revelation (5:4-10). He's the Lion and the Lamb. He's the Alpha and the Omega. He's the Savior of the world! All hail King Jesus! Your relationship with Him is the oil this world needs! Your history with God will be brought to the forefront as, "creation waits in eager expectation for the children of God to be revealed." (Romans 8:19 NIV)

Turn all your attention to Jesus while there's still time to gather the oil for your lamps. When He returns, it will be too little too late if you're not ready. Nobody else can go and gather it for you. Only you can do it. Will you be found ready?

"Now it happened as they went that He entered a certain village; and a certain woman named Martha welcomed Him into her house. And she had a sister called Mary, who also sat at Jesus' feet and heard His word. But Martha was distracted with much serving, and she approached Him and said, "Lord, do You not care that my sister has left me to serve alone? Therefore tell her to help me." And Jesus answered and said to her, "Martha, Martha, you are worried and troubled about many things. But one thing is needed, and Mary has chosen that good part, which will not be taken away from her."" (Luke 10:38-42 NKJV)

What was the *one thing* Jesus was talking about? The Bible tells us that Mary was sitting at the feet of Jesus listening to every word He said. The Bible makes it clear that if Jesus says anything, it is more important than anything else we could possibly comprehend or hear from anyone else. Jesus literally says, there is only one thing that is needed. If He says something that profound, then something inside of us should change everything about the way we do life. Rearranging our days, time, and freedoms to readily invest ourselves into engaging with Him is a necessity.

If *He* says anything, it means everything because the

audience of one matters the most. He said that one thing was needed and because Mary chose it, that investment would not be taken away from her. Let's stop looking to every other voice as if it mattered more than His. Yes, the world is crazy and unprecedented, and I do not disagree. There is political turmoil, injustices, suffering, health concerns, and a plethora of other anxieties that one can think about. If you put all of those things to the side, do you see Jesus? If you cannot, then you must get to His feet, turn off the other chatter and hang on the words of Jesus as if your life depended on it. You must run to Him and shout "Jesus, you are what I long for. You are the one thing I need." This is where the oil of intimacy is birthed from. We must get to His feet and tell Him, "I care about what you care about, and I want you today and every day." You must turn your attention to the Lord. No matter where you are in life, call out to Jesus and receive the Son of God's mercy and provision. When you ask Him to "give me today my daily bread," you can be sure He will provide all of the sustenance needed for living.

"At that time his voice shook the earth, but now he has promised, "Once more I will shake not only the earth but also the heavens." The words "once more" indicate the removing of what can be shaken—that is, created things—so that what cannot be shaken may remain. Therefore, since we are receiving a kingdom that cannot be shaken, let us be thankful, and so worship God

acceptably with reverence and awe, for our "God is a consuming fire."" (Hebrews 12:26-28)

It is dangerously easy to be swayed in our generation from social media, news channels, movies, television, and the culture that's all around us. These enticing forces, driven by the spirit of the world, relentlessly contend for our spirit and thinking, so keeping our focus is more critical than ever. If we're driving and take our eyes off the road, the vehicle will veer in the direction we're looking, and we could easily get up-close-and-personal with a ditch! As believers, we lose sight of our way when we lose sight of His Words and begin to speak our own...

For example, when we complain or grumble against circumstances, it rises against the reality of what God is speaking into our lives. Instead, let's *embrace* our hidden seasons rather than complain about them. It's those very moments when He is refining us in His refiners fire.

What Jesus does in your life cannot be shaken. It can't be shaken by what the media says. His kingdom cannot be shaken by what a family member said. His kingdom cannot be shaken by someone making a negative comment. His kingdom cannot be shaken from however He's tailor making you, fashioning you, forming you, and anointing you in your hidden places of pursuit of our great God. When we try to build what we want, I can guarantee it will be shaken. But His Kingdom shall not be shaken, and it will remain in your life, through your life, and from your life for a world that desperately needs the Gospel of Jesus Christ.

He is looking for His chosen ones in this season while he is trimming the masses to those that really believe and obey His words. As He trims all of the extra that we have added to our Christian living, He is establishing something in His kingdom that cannot be shaken. Where is He doing this? In you and me. He is doing it in the lives of believers. He did it in the lives of the three thousand people who believed in what Peter said. He did it with the lives of the three hundred who followed Gideon. He did it with the thousands following Him for free handouts, and He did it with His inner circle of disciples. He is doing it in the lives of whoever is willing to put the desires of Jesus above their own personal desires.

He is your audience of one.

4

EMBRACE YOUR SEASON

As this booklet draws to a close in its final chapter, I pray your heart is being stirred and awakened to refocusing your attention on the One in your audience that matters more than any other. I hope you are sensing the sweet desire to reshift your priorities, to reshape your reality into His, and to reawaken the destiny He has written about your life before the world ever began. Psalm 139:16 says, "You saw me before I was born. Every day of my life was recorded in your book. Every moment was laid out before a single day had passed." To think He knew every day of what you'd walk through, and He loves you. He wrote your plans to prosper and succeed, and He even created a cheerleading section in Heaven called the "great cloud of witnesses," while even Jesus Himself intercedes for you.

With all of this said, many will take the steps to begin walking into this new season of resolve with the Lord and find themselves asking the question of why when it suddenly gets hard. I want to challenge you to embrace your season with the Lord! No matter if He stays with you and leads you in the valley of the shadow of death (Psalm 23:4), in the fields of harvest (Matthew 28:19-20), in the fiery tests and trials (1 Peter 4:12-13), or in the joys of victory (1 John 5:4), that your heart would be fully His in a steady embrace of your season.

Among the most beautiful facets of following God, is the profound obscurity unique to His ways. Look at Elijah the prophet, whom God used to glorify His name with an extraordinary roster of miracles. For example, Elijah's prayers sealed the heavens so they would not bring rain (1 Kings 17:1, James 5:17). Following that, not only did he raise a child from the dead in 1 Kings 17:22, but he also called down fire from Heaven during a showdown with the prophets of Baal in 1 Kings 18:38 (to name just a few). Perhaps the most remarkable thing about Elijah, however, is that there is no backstory describing the life he lived that shaped him into the man of God he became — he simply emerged out of "seemingly nothing" as one who stood before the Lord God of Israel in 1 Kings 17:1.

Luke 1:80 describes John the Baptist the same way, explaining that, "...And he lived in the wilderness until he began his public ministry to Israel." John was given to anonymity and content to live in the wilderness until the Lord released him into "public ministry to Israel."

It was the same for Jesus! He began His ministry at 30 years old. Jesus worked as a simple carpenter, running the family business before his launch into the spotlight. In fact, little is even mentioned about Jesus outside of His famous birth and childhood visit to the temple.

When God looks at a man, it quickly becomes clear that He forms godly character in secret and sees a beauty in obscurity that He treasures. It is a key building block that He often shapes those He intends to use in the secret place. Daniel 2:22 says, "He reveals deep and mysterious things and knows what lies hidden in darkness, though he is surrounded by light." God often places us in the hidden places so that He can reveal His marvelous light away from the limelight. It's those who are famous in this place, who often carry His exploits and make His name famous in the earth.

Unfortunately, what we miss so often is when He tucks us away, He's offering us the opportunity to be hidden and the grace to pursue the depths of His heart *in secret*. We tend to shun the secret place, and instead, we default to a desire to be promoted because we long to be seen — perhaps to share what God has given us rather than sharing in God Himself. If we could embrace that season and treasure it, we would realize it was what He was after in us all along! We often look for something to happen in His presence, all the while forgetting that His presence is Him being present. He's the prize, and He is what is happening!

The story of Esther reveals this fruit as God groomed her for greatness in the solitude of her day-to-day life. And in the throes of her anonymity, Mordecai challenged her with the words, "...Yet who knows whether you have come to the kingdom for such a time as this" (Esther 4:14 NKJV). In that crucial hour, Esther had become ripe to fulfill the destiny God had appointed her to. She fell to her knees, fasting and praying for a word from Heaven to save her people, and God, who ripened her in secret, set her apart and rewarded her to bear its fruit openly.

In this hour, in this season, at this moment, it is too important to neglect your times in the secret place. What He shapes and forms in us, is the fruit this world desperately needs. They will taste and see the goodness of God through you, me, the global body of Christ that's prepared itself away from the noise. What is revealed in secret, will be made known in season!

I want to encourage you in the final words of this book, to stop looking at what the crowds are saying. I want to encourage you to prepare your life for your audience of one and to think what He wants most in and through your life. I want to encourage you to take a look at restructuring your day to do the one thing that is needed most, listening to Jesus. This is what will change our world, what will change our nation, what will change our families, and what will change you and me; a blood bought Bride who knows who she is and hangs on His precious words, and a Bride who immediately responds to His leading. A Bride who allows Jesus to be our AUDIENCE OF ONE is the only thing that the gates of Hell will not prevail against (see Matthew 16:18). What we prepare for Him is the only thing that will last.

What you decide to do with your time from this moment will determine eternity for you and for those around you. Truly embrace your season, and allow God to fashion, form, and shape you. Listen to Him, and do what He says. This is the only way to love Him. John 14:21 says, "Those who accept my commandments and obey them are the ones who love me. And because they love me, my Father will love them. And I will love them and reveal myself to each of them." What He reveals to you in secret will change the destiny of your life and everyone else. Let's give Jesus our everything. Let's pour our love on Him. Let's live our lives not for the applause of the people around us but in a unified heartbeat with a God who loves us. No matter what may come, may He be the only audience that matters.

Jesus, I love you.

CALEB WAMPLER travels around the world with a burning passion to see the lost in the darkest corners of the earth hear the life-changing message of the gospel. His life has been significantly marked by supernatural encounters from an early age and he desires to bring the body of Christ into the deeper things of the faith. Whether he's in a remote village on the other side of the earth, or a church in America, his heart is that everyone would encounter the Living God. Caleb's life of faith, echo's the prayer of Jesus, "Your Kingdom come, your will be done, on earth as it is in heaven."

Caleb's continual message is intimacy and relationship with Jesus Christ. He is an evangelist that not only brings the lost to their Savior but teaches them to go into the inner chambers and experience a love-relationship with their bridegroom. The Wampler's minister in churches around the world, do in-depth teachings, impartation services, crusades, and operate in signs, wonders, and miracles.

Caleb and his wife Harmonee currently reside in the Orlando, FL area with their four children, Elisha, Eliana, Caden, and Jeremiah. At the time this book was written, their ministry has already reached over one million people with the message of Jesus. They share the gospel on TV stations throughout the middle east and have a podcast called 'Awaken The Wonder' on the Charisma Podcast Network.

For more information or to follow up, visit:

WWW.CALEBWAMPLER.COM

To hear a special word from the author, Evangelist Caleb Wampler, see QR code below:

Made in the USA
Columbia, SC
25 August 2022